twilight saga

new moon

THE SCORE
MUSIC BY ALEXANDRE DESPLAT

SUMMIT ENTERTAINMENT PRESENTS "THE TWILIGHT SAGA: NEW MOON"

A TEMPLE HILL PRODUCTION IN ASSOCIATION WITH MAVERICK / IMPRINT AND SUNSWEPT ENTERTAINMENT KRISTEN STEWART ROBERT PATTINSON TAYLOR LAUTNER ASHLEY GREENE RACHELLE LEFEVRE BILLY BURKE PETER FACINELLI ELIZABETH REASER NIKKI REED KELLAN LUTZ JACKSON RATHBONE ANNA KENDRICK WITH MICHAEL SHEEN AND DAKOTA FANNING CASTING BY JOSEPH MIDDLETON, C.S.A. MUSIC BY ALEXANDRE DESPLAT MUSIC SUPERVISOR ALEXANDRA PATSAVAS COSTUME DESIGNER TISH MONAGHAN EDITOR PETER LAMBERT PRODUCTION DESIGNER DAVID BRISBIN DIRECTOR OF PHOTOGRAPHY JAVIER AGUIRRESAROBE CO-PRODUCER BILL BANNERMAN EXECUTIVE PRODUCERS MARTY BOWEN GREG MOORADIAN MARK MORGAN GUY OSEARY PRODUCED BY WYCK GODFREY KAREN ROSENFELT BASED ON THE NOVEL "NEW MOON" BY STEPHENIE MEYER SCREENPLAY BY MELISSA ROSENBERG DIRECTED BY CHRIS WEITZ

PG-13 PARENTS STRONGLY CAUTIONED
Some Material May Be Inappropriate for Children Under 13
Some Violence and Action

DOLBY

11.20.09
www.newmoonthemovie.com

ISBN 978-1-4234-7550-7

HAL•LEONARD®
CORPORATION
7777 W. BLUEMOUND RD. P.O. BOX 13819 MILWAUKEE, WI 53213

In Australia Contact:
Hal Leonard Australia Pty. Ltd.
4 Lentara Court
Cheltenham, Victoria, 3192 Australia
Email: ausadmin@halleonard.com.au

NEW MOON

Composed by
ALEXANDRE DESPLAT

Moderately fast

With pedal

ROMEO & JULIET

Composed by
ALEXANDRE DESPLAT

Moderately slow

EDWARD LEAVES

Composed by
ALEXANDER DESPLAT

Moderately slow, expressively

Ped.

VOLTURI WALTZ

Composed by
ALEXANDRE DESPLAT

I NEED YOU

Composed by
ALEXANDRE DESPLAT

MEMORIES OF EDWARD

Composed by
ALEXANDRE DESPLAT

Moderately

With pedal

ALMOST A KISS

Composed by
ALEXANDRE DESPLAT

Moderately slow

ADRENALINE

Composed by
ALEXANDER DESPLAT

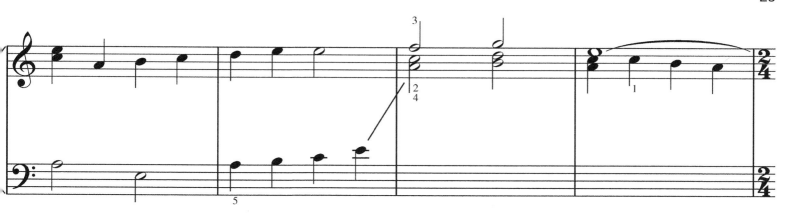

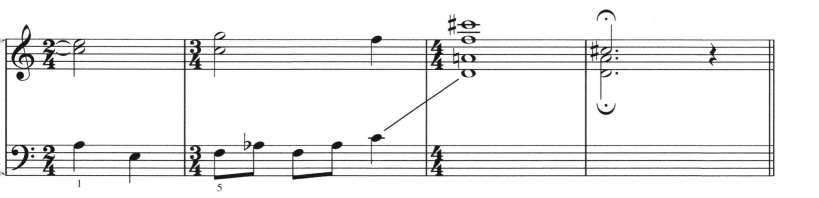

Faster, steadily

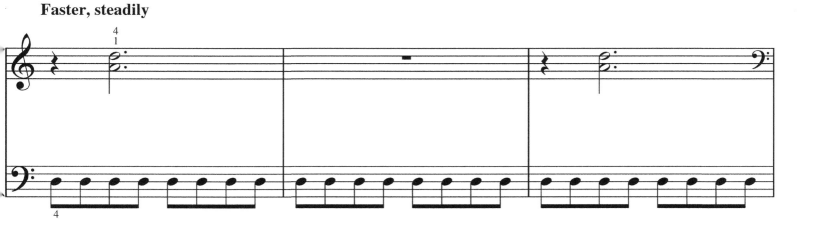

R.H. over L.H.

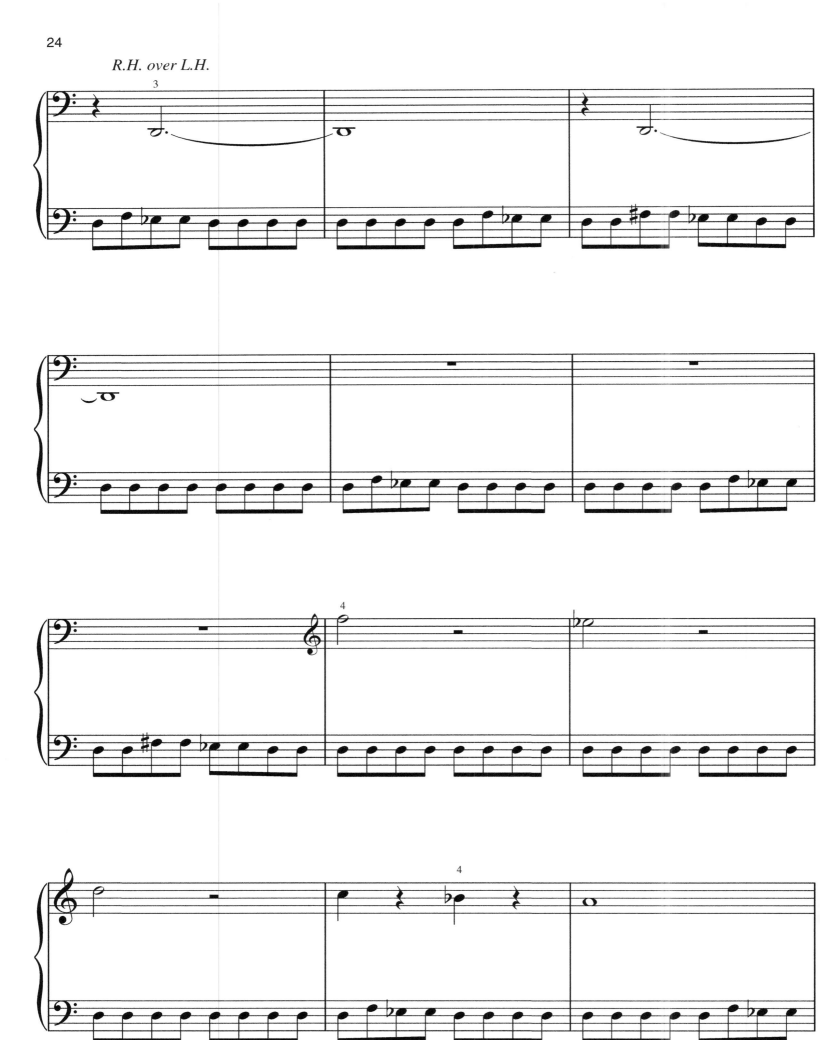

R.H. over L.H.

DREAMCATCHER

Composed by
ALEXANDRE DESPLAT

TO VOLTERRA

Composed by
ALEXANDER DESPLAT

Slowly, with freedom

With pedal

THE CULLENS

Composed by
ALEXANDRE DESPLAT

Moderately slow, expressively

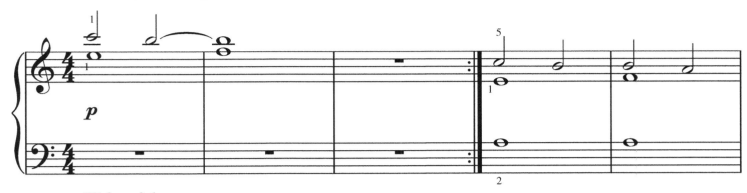

p

With pedal

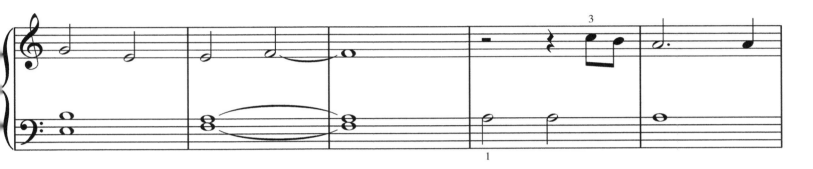

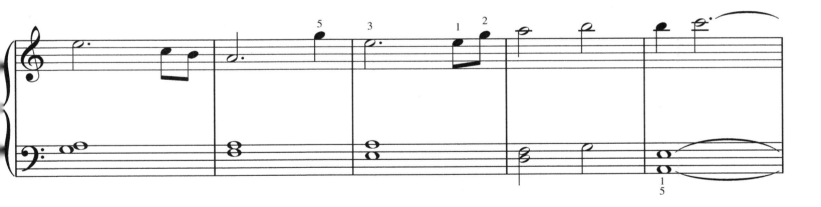

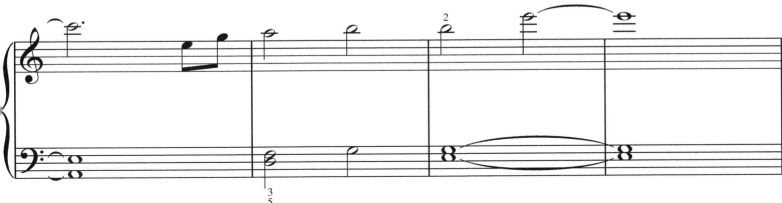

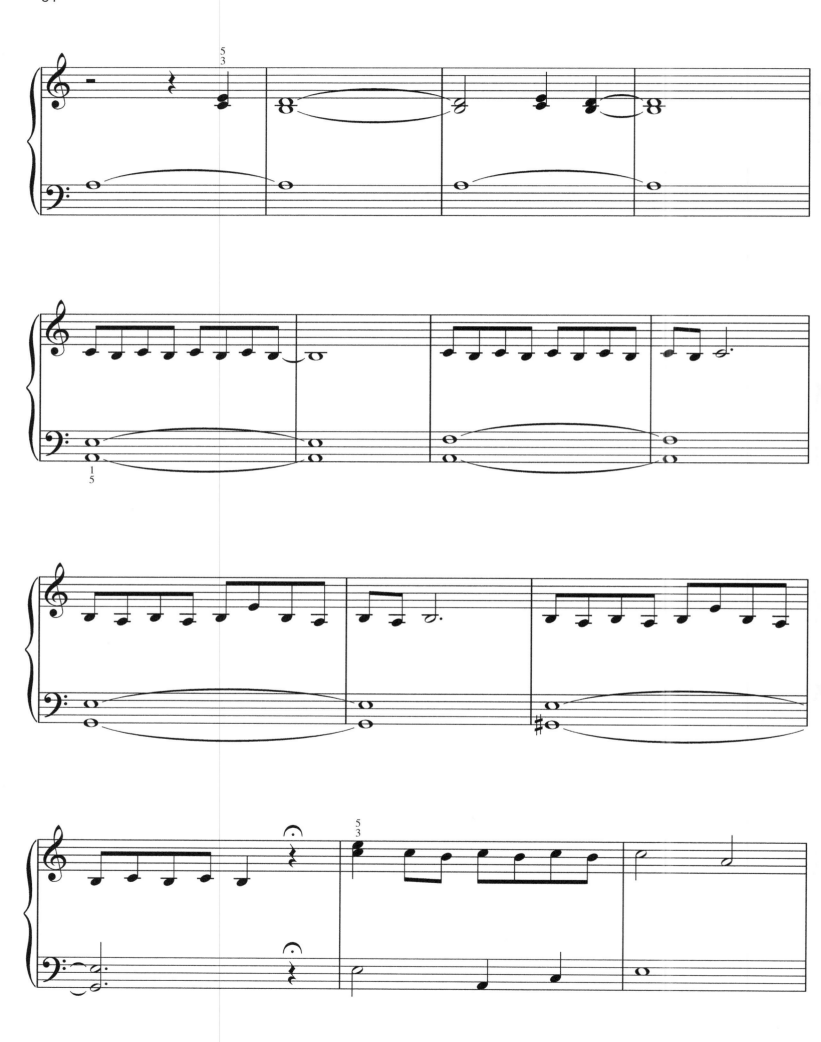

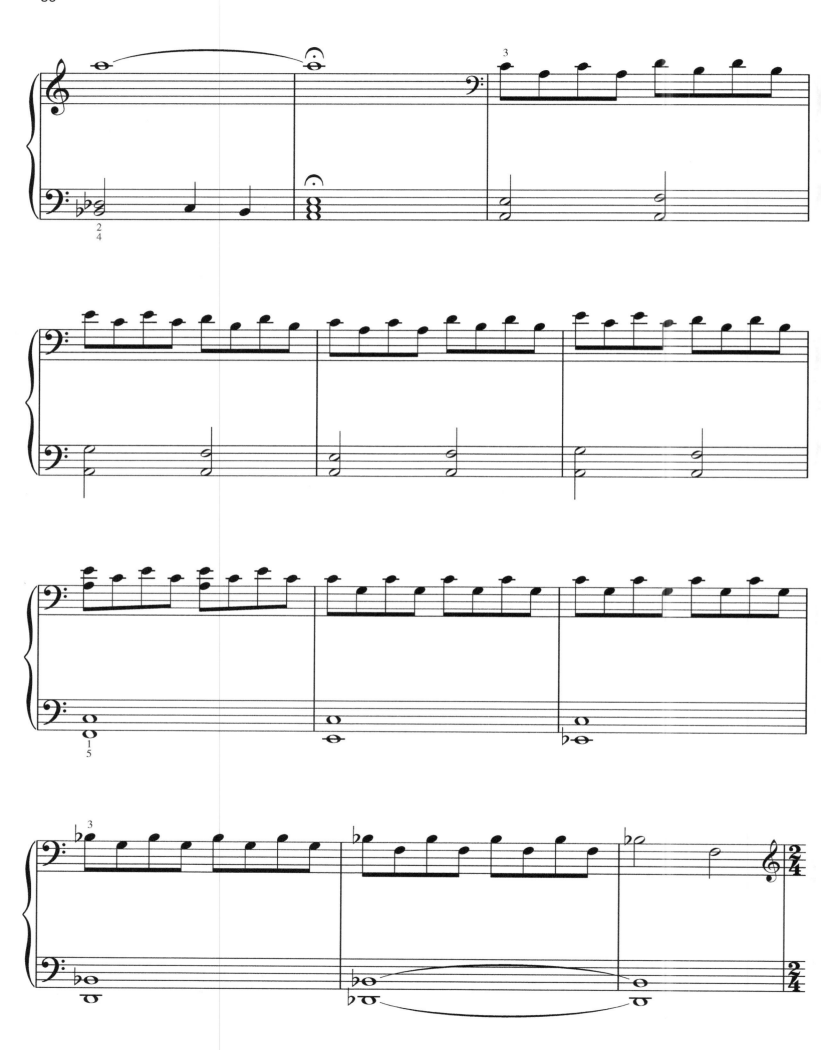

YOU'RE ALIVE

Composed by
ALEXANDER DESPLAT

Moderately slow

With pedal

MARRY ME, BELLA

Composed by
ALEXANDRE DESPLAT

Moderately

Play 4 times

With pedal

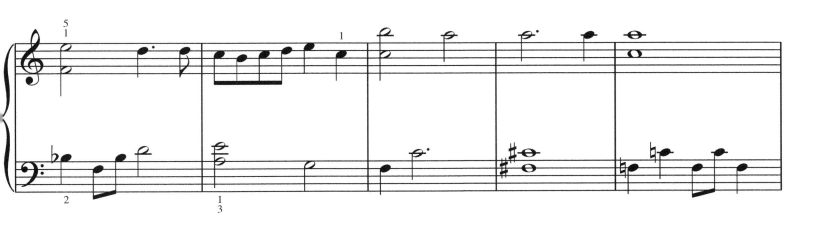

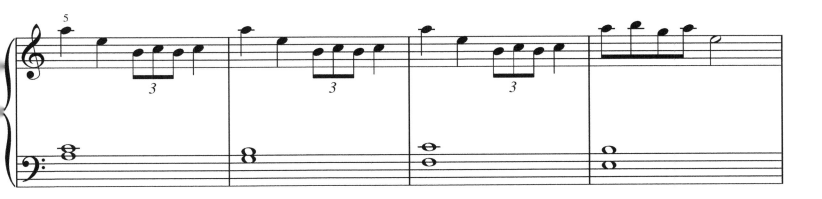

FULL MOON

Composed by
ALEXANDRE DESPLAT